MAXWELL RIDDLE Writing in The World's Largest All Breed Dog Magazine; **Dog World,** (October 1985, page 41)

"If you have spent a fortune for a dog which you can't housetrain (or one that costs even five cents) you should buy this very startling book . . . The method works for just weaned pups and for old dogs which have resisted training for years . . . Breeders would do well to give copies with each puppy they sell . . ."

BILL KOEHLER Chief Animal Trainer at Disney Studios for 20 years and author of many great dog training books (Howell Book House)

"Want to housebreak your dog? Dr. Marjorie Smith and Mother Nature can help you. It's all in this little book. Dr. Smith's unique solution to the problem springs from her deep knowledge of the dog's physiology and character. I've seen her concept work. Your success with the method might seem like a miracle, but it will be only natural. So universally needed . . . **I unequivocally endorse the book.***"*

JOB MICHAEL EVANS (Dog Fancy Magazine, July 1985, page 20)

"If books on house training cause you to smile, remember that for many dog owners this is no laughing matter . . . YOU CAN TEACH YOUR DOG TO ELIMINATE ON COMMAND sports a no-frills title and the text gets right to the point . . . Dr. Smith had contributed an important essay to an evolving area of canine studies. She has taken on an area of canine training that baffles many dog owners and has made the process understandable to owners and certainly simpler for dogs.

ZOE SWANAGON — CANINE BEHAVIOR CENTER, SEATTLE, WASHINGTON ("When All Else Fails You CAN HOUSEBREAK THAT DOG" page 18-19)

"For the first time EVER, there is a book available on the subject of teaching your dog to eliminate on command. It is probably the most important book you will ever own if you are a dog owner, no matter how long you have lived with the dog . . . The book is by Dr. Marge Smith, and is appropriately called 'Eliminate on Command' ".

Eliminate on Command / i

Published with permission of
The Foundation for Applied Studies of Animal Behavior
Chicago, Illinois

Special Edition
First Printing, 1984
Second Printing, 1986
Third Printing, 1991
All rights reserved.
© 1984, Smith-Sager Publications
ISBN 0-9617649-0-2

You Can Teach Your Dog to
ELIMINATE ON COMMAND

by
Dr. M. L. Smith

with drawings by
Syd Stibbard

Table of Contents

4 / Eliminate on Command

PROLOGUE

I have a fine bookkeeper at my office who is now nearly 80 years old. Her little dog Daisy is pretty vigorous and agile—more so than her owner—and this is especially true on cold, wet winter mornings when arthritis and old bones are reluctant to negotiate the steps from their mobile home, across the rough gravel and irregular muddy ground, to Daisy's preferred spot; but Dorothy dutifully walks her dog three or four times a day for Daisy's exercise and elimination. Daisy is small and active, and gets most of her exercise jumping up and down from the furniture and rushing about the house, so long walks in the winter rain are often unnecessary. But Daisy, like many dogs, has learned to "walk her owner" a long way before deigning to complete her elimination.

When Dorothy was recuperating from a slip on her icy steps last year, and so confined for a few days, she almost worried herself to death about Daisy and her walks.

In just half an hour, I was able to explain to Dorothy how to get Daisy to piddle and poop on command—a technique we now call "PPC"—and although she had never had to train a dog before, she felt the situation made it worth the effort. Most of our discussion was dedicated to overcoming her "Yes, but—" objections, and to giving her confidence that something so simple could work.

Less than ten days later, she informed me gleefully that, "It worked!" She could open the door, give her chosen command, "Bid-a-Bet", as Daisy went down the steps (alone!), eliminated at once, and came back quickly on her own initiative. If the morning was rainy and cold, only the dog got wet, and not too wet at that. Dorothy was thrilled and grateful. She was able to get through the remaining slippery winter days without further injury, and continued to cheer up our office with her wonderful sense of humor.

The year before this, my sister had called and described her new dog Duffy, who had to be walked and **walked** and *walked* to obtain adequate elimination. There were sand storms then in Tucson, and these kept her from staying out as long as Duffy required. I told her about PPC over the telephone, and it soon was working for her, too.

I began to realize that this simple procedure would help many people out of similar troubles, while creating many more happy dog homes. I do not know how many dogs end up in the "gas chambers" of animal control facilities because of unsolved elimination problems, but I do know that the number is staggering.

Many cities have new laws requiring owners to clean up dog stools at once, and when the dog picks the area, this can make matters surprisingly difficult! There are few enough city apartments or rental units these days which allow pets, and many of the objections derive from elimination problems—both indoors and out.

Using PPC, we rehabilitated a nine-year-old Afghan who had lived kenneled since birth. Each time someone had tried to give the dog an indoor home, he would be returned to the kennel in a few weeks because he would continue to eliminate inside the house. All the usual techniques for correcting this problem had failed when an Afghan-lover from one of our Shepherd House classes decided to take the dog home "on trial." She immediately introduced PPC, gaining substantial control of the problem in a week. The dog was completely housebroken in three months, and trained in Novice Obedience at the same time. A beautiful problem dog with a partial "kennel syndrome" is now a pleasant and happy companion in a loving home.

PPC can also help you to understand just how great a teacher **you** can be. Once you know the rules by which your dog learns this particularly useful pattern, you may be encouraged to go further, teaching your dog many other useful things that will give both of you pleasure.

There is a marvelous additional bonus available to you, the trainer, through this book —one which may be unique among all dog training techniques:

If you normally walk your dog for elimination and exercise, the only extra time you will have to spend teaching PPC to your dog is the time it takes you to read these pages!

All of the actual teaching will take place during the normal walks you must take anyway, and furthermore, you'll have plenty of leisure to watch birds or clouds, or do your jogging, because the **entire training time needed to accomplish your goal is less than five minutes during the entire week.** Nevertheless, the dog still comes out ahead in regard to time spent, because he doesn't have to read the book!

NOTES

Appendix C beginning on page 77 outlines some specific rules I have found to be most helpful for people teaching their dogs. The rules listed there are only those which were used in the construction of the PPC teaching regime; I am including them to help you understand the principles behind this training which have a more universal application for use with the dog.

Throughout this book, I have used the word "sound" to indicate a verbal command, but a visual signal or a touch signal would, of course, work just as surely.

And although a dog is an "it" to many people, this is certainly not true for me, and I have used the pronoun "he" when referring to "the dog" regardless of sex.

This small treatise is devoted to giving all dogs and dog owners a smoother, happier and easier life together.

M. L. Smith, M.D.
Billihill Farm
Friday Harbor, Washington

Dedicated to Daisy and Duffy.
in memory of
Heber Bill, CDX.

"Here we go"

PIDDLE AND POOP ON COMMAND

POSITIVE
POTTY
CONTROL

P P C

18 / Eliminate on Command

THE PRINCIPLE

WOULD you like your dog to eliminate on command?

Hundreds of dog owners who have been through our Shepherd House obedience classes in the Chicagoland area over the past 13 years have been enjoying this luxury. It is one of the simplest things to teach a dog, it works at all ages above six weeks, and creates a wonderful life-long convenience for both the owner and the dog.

Many people have inadvertently taught PPC, discovering that when they say "so and so" the dog always "does his business."

This book will tell them how they did it!

Imagine the benefits to you and your pet:

- On a cold rainy night
- When visiting in strange places
- When introducing a dog to a new area
- When you want to confine your dog's wastes to a certain specific area
- When you must rush off to a meeting after a fast dinner for both you and your dog
- Before entering an obedience competition ring
- When you must change your dog's routine for any reason
- Before caging a dog for an airline trip

There are many more benefits of PPC, of course, and you can be taking advantage of them just ten days from now.

You can establish a conditioned reflex in your dog by associating a special sound with the beginning of both urination and defecation. Fifty to 75 repetitions are needed in order to establish a functional result. When the repetitions have been adequately carried out, the sound itself will cause the dog to "feel an urge" and respond to it by eliminating anything contained in his bladder or bowel at the moment.

From then on, whenever you say the trigger word, even at a strange time or place, your dog will do his best to eliminate almost immediately.

That's the general idea. Now let's discuss the details of this conditioning work so that you can begin the training today.

The process is so simple that you may be wondering why there are so many pages in this book. The reasons are:

- The dog can actively respond to his own thought 7 to 10 times faster than can the human.

- New associations are accurately made in the dog's mind between events which occur exactly together—simultaneously.

Thus we slower humans must generally plan ahead when wishing to teach the dog a new trick.

The chapters which follow are designed to get you ahead of the dog—armed with a tiny, perfect plan you can execute at the dog's "proper instant." With this advance planning based on your careful observation, you'll be able to achieve perfect rapid conditioning and avoid time wasting errors.

PREREQUISITES

THERE are four prerequisites:

1. The puppy should be more than six weeks of age when you begin to teach PPC.

PPC alone cannot housebreak your puppy, but it can help you enormously in your housebreaking efforts and greatly speed the development of reliable housebreaking patterns.

It is also true that the puppy from 7 to 11 weeks of age probably will be trained to eliminate on command in considerably less than a week.

*"Now **I** guess **I** have to trespass to cleanup!"*

2. The dog must have places to go that he understands are "okay," and he should be eliminating regularly in those places.

It would be severely unfair for your dog to have no places where he could eliminate in comfort and with your approval. Elimination is, of course, necessary to his life.

For example, if you have just moved from the country to the city and your dog thinks he cannot eliminate on a paved surface, you will have to find an area where he feels free to eliminate before you start this specialized PPC training.

You will just have to bear with **his** chosen places until you have finished your teaching of PPC.

After the dog has been taught PPC in an area where he eliminates comfortably without emotional strain or stress, it will be easy to introduce him to new areas where you wish to have him eliminate at **your** convenience.

3. It must be "okay" with the dog for you to be in the area with him during his elimination.

Since you are going to use a trigger word or sound at a very special moment, it is necessary that you be within easy hearing distance while the dog is eliminating. You also need to be able to see exactly what is going on with the dog at the time when you will give your special command word.

Since a number of adult dogs who have yards of their own or are allowed to be free out of doors are often quite "modest," and will go to an area out of the owner's sight for their elimination, it may be necessary for them to be conditioned to a human presence.

To assist you with more details in this regard:

*See **Appendix A** for dogs who want to eliminate only when they are **out-of-sight**.*

*See **Appendix B** for dogs who want to eliminate only when **off-leash**.*

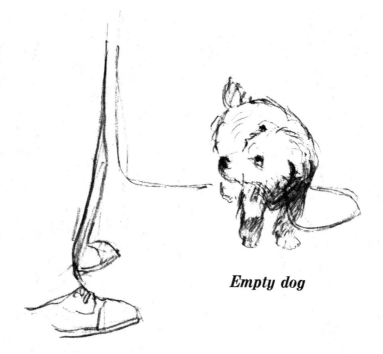

Empty dog

4. The act of elimination can take place only if there is some urine in the bladder or feces in the bowel.

I know this seems all too obvious, but if you find you are walking an "empty dog," you will certainly want to discover the reason!

Following

Summary Of Prerequisites

Any normal, healthy dog over six weeks of age can be taught PPC if he has a comfortable place to eliminate and will let you be in the area with him while he is eliminating.

Bid-a-bet
Bid-a-bet
Bid-a-bet

Dumpty
Dumpty
Dum . . .

P P C
P P C
P P C

Can-do
Can-do
Can-do

Tango
Tango

Sis Boom
Sis Boom

Go do it
Go do it

CHOOSING THE COMMAND

IT is best to choose a short sound or 'trigger' word—two or three syllables at the most—for the elimination command. It should be an unusual sound or phrase—not a word or sound which you and your family would use in every-day conversation about the house, or out of doors. It can be a nonsense syllable or sound, a word in a foreign language, or any other special choice you'd like, such as:

potty-go	hit it
hi-castle	do it
guy-go	par-tee

PPC! ??

Some commonly used words have been "hurry up" and "okay" and "outside," but these can be quite unsatisfactory: they are so much a part of everyone's conversation that the dog can get hundreds of unintended and misleading signals!

Other sounds you may wish to avoid are those used in standard dog obedience and trial work: heel, sit, stay, come, down, lay, free, kennel, stand, go, go out, find it, over, back, fetch, hold, give, get it. Most of these you will notice are single syllable words, and although the list is long, people have had little difficulty choosing a distinctly different set of sounds for elimination commands.

The dog's attention and sound discrimination will best be served by using words with clear vowel sounds and sharp-sounding consonants. For example, the soft vowels and consonants in a sound like "paw paw" would be hard for the dog to distinguish if near a busy city street, while the command "key key" would be much clearer. (PPC used as a trigger word obeys the rules of the vowel and consonant sounds.) The PPC technique is most useful in times and places when all is definitely **not** tranquil and unhurried, but when wind, hail, lightning, and thunder may all be competing for your dog's attention at one time, while you want him to attend only to the very necessary things, get them done, and return to the house! So take some time and choose this command well. It will become a sound that will give you great satisfaction from now on!

During the teaching process, do not use the dog's name at any time in association with the command. You do not want to alert the dog to you. You want his whole mind on **his** business and his own personal sense of urgency. Therefore none of the sounds that you make should interfere in any way with the dog's attention to his internal sensations.

When the teaching has been completed, however, you will often need to alert the dog to you by using his name before the command.

The final important sounds to avoid are those which would be similar to the dog's name, or the names of members of your family. Planning ahead properly is clearly needed in choosing a command.

Practicing

If you have made a choice, but find, as did one student recently, that you can't remember your word at the moment of need—or if for any other reason you decide your first choice is not to your liking—don't hesitate to select a new command and simply abandon the less desirable one. It will not delay you very much since you will probably discover the problem while you are practicing your timing.

The shorter the command sound, the more times you can repeat it during a single episode of stance and sphincter opening. This has an obvious advantage: the more times you can say the word with each elimination, the sooner you will have said it the proper number of times to achieve your end point—50 to 75 times in a week.

The same command must be used for both urination and moving the bowel. There is no way **you** can know which thing the dog needs to do first! So the command, in the finished training process, must include both acts.

Establishing the Proper Moment

For Inserting The Command

FOR a few walks, watch your dog carefully for each of the actions listed below. Practice repeating your command word silently, under your breath, until you have your timing well matched to his.

In order for you to isolate those specific moments when the command sounds can be most effectively repeated, we'll pretend to turn on a very slow-motion camera and record many dogs' eliminations.

When we play back our finished film, we'll see evidence of some or all of the following:

1. A sense of urgency on the dog's part: anxiety or inattentiveness to surrounding events due to internal attention; a consciousness of sensation in his bladder or bowel.

2. A sniffing pattern.

3. A circling pattern.

4. A normal stance or body attitude for elimination—you must become familiar with the stance that is unique to the sex and breed of your dog.

5. The actual initiating act is the opening of the bladder or bowel sphincter. (A sphincter is a circular muscle which closes a natural opening.)

6. At sphincter opening time, the powerful muscles of the bladder or bowel wall will be contracting to push out the necessary waste.

7. Emptying of the bladder or bowel, which is followed by

8. Sphincter closing,

9. Muscular relaxation, and

10. Leaving the area.

The exact sphincter opening time with its maximum force of contraction of the eliminating muscles is very important to your command. Actually, the sphincter opening and the initiating muscular contraction overlap one another in time.

Softly repeat your command during stages 4, 5 and 6. Once you begin the sound, don't stop until step 6 is finished.

We pinpoint the **end** of the sphincter opening time by watching for the waste to appear in volume and with force (7).

When the dog's elimination is in process, stop your trigger phrase. You do **not** want to associate the trigger with the **end** of elimination, when the sphincter must close and the other muscles will all relax. Stop your command word when the dog is **actually** eliminating. You may, very usefully, change to very soft praise words, inserting two or three "good dogs" as elimination is going on; **but be sure to stop your praise before the sphincter closes.**

Sniffing

Circling

Stance

When the dog takes up his stance, get close enough so that the leash is loose—not tugging, on his collar. A tight collar can detract from the attention he is placing on his sensations and your voice.

Very small dogs, when eliminating, may hardly appear to be doing so. A female Dachshund can rather quickly squat and eliminate before you realize that she has done so. The male dog of any breed who eliminates his urine without leg lifting may fool you also, and be through before you know it.

So, for Positive Potty Control, you need to plan ahead and be ready with your soft command at the dog's moment of maximum urgency. At that moment the muscles of the entire animal—voluntary and involuntary—are all engaged in the sphincter opening phase.

Your newly-chosen command must be imprinted simultaneously with the sphincter opening events in order to achieve perfect and rapid conditioning.

Ready?

The
Perfect
Moment

Silence

More About Conditioning Details

Since the dog clearly relates and associates events which occur **simultaneously** with one another, you must be just as accurate in the timing of your praise as you are in timing new commands.

For example, if your dog is acting shy about meeting a stranger at the front door and you want to give him courage, you may talk softly and pat him, perhaps pushing him forward or pulling him forward with his collar, saying soft and encouraging words. As you pull him forward, **he will be pulling back with all his muscles.** The dog will consider your "soft talk" as praise for his pulling back, as well as his present shy feelings and attitude, and he will gradually appear more and more shy. In his mind you will have praised him for showing shyness.!

The same type of sequence applies for the dog showing aggression at the door. Soft talk, patting, restraint—which you think will help calm the dog down—will be interpreted by him as praise for his attitude, which includes lunging **toward** your caller, and he will become more and more aggressive and harder to handle.

Watch what your puppy or dog is actually, actively **doing** when you give **any** order to him, or praise him. If his muscles and attitude are engaged in activity opposite to that which you desire, don't repeat your command over and over. It will obviously only condition the dog to do **exactly** what you do **not** want.

The dog does not "naturally" understand English, especially when the meaning of a word is presented to him in backwards fashion. I watched a man chasing his happy, running-away golden retriever for 15 minutes one afternoon. He shouted "Rusty, Come!" 50-75 times during a long wild chase. I know he had no idea he was making matters worse with every futile call. I drove away feeling very sad as the dog and man disappeared into the woods.

Study the
- commands
- inadvertent praisings
- planned praisings

you and your family members or friends are giving your dog.

Look carefully at the need to provide praisings **while** the dog is doing the perfect thing. If you cannot provide the correct information at the proper moment, it is better to wait for a new chance, for which you have planned ahead and are ready.

Checklist of Preparedness

yes

- Is the dog more than six weeks old? . . . . . . ☐

- Do we have a comfortable place for
his elimination? One that he likes? . . . . ☐

- Do I know when he usually needs
to go out? . . . . ☐

- Can I see my dog when he takes up
his special stance? . . . . ☐

  When his sphincter opens? . . . . ☐

  When the stream starts? . . . . ☐

  When the stool appears at the anus? . . ☐

- Have I chosen a good word or sound? . . . . . ☐

- Have I practiced soft praise during the
above times to get my dog gently used to
the sound of my voice at those special
moments? . . . . ☐

When you can answer "yes" to all of the above questions you are ready to condition the dog to your chosen command. Five to seven days from now you can have a beautiful reflex built in.

*You're bound to miss
a few chances*

Questions and Answers

Q. Do I have to see and use every elimination?

A. No. You are bound to miss some probably, but the more you **can** do, the sooner the good results.

Q. As the first teacher, do I have to walk the dog every time he's walked this week?

A. No. A couple of times a day will be enough. If you can make it three times, it may go faster, of course.

**Another way to miss
the moment!**

Q. Do I have to repeat the word 50 times for urine and 50 times for bowel movements?

A. The problem with this question is that none of us is certain of the ideal number. We haven't counted our repetitions with perfect accuracy. Our dogs have surprised us in too many ways during a week of walks, and we lose track of the numbers. Pavlov and other scientists have said that 50 repetitions are needed, but there is some variation among the authorities. Our own method has worked so infallibly that we have simply ignored the numerical details and accepted our successes. Most dogs have a stool twice a day. If I use my trigger phrase correctly three to four times for every stool for a week, I would get a total of about 45 repetitions that week for stool training.

Some kind of overlap seems to occur with the two types of elimination, because the dog who has a stool only once a day is usually just as well-conditioned by the end of the week as the one who has more. As I do not wish to fly in the face of science (!), I will just sidestep the issue in favor of the success you are going to have if you ignore this problem altogether!

(After Zeno posed his impertinent paradox, it took centuries for mathematicians to find a way of proving the hare **could** overtake the tortoise, and that the arrow **could** reach the target!)

Q. I walk two dogs at once. How can I teach them both?

A. My suggestion would be to teach the calmer dog first for your own practice, and choose a separate command for each dog. Then you won't need to walk the dogs separately. It will take you two weeks, one week for each dog, but you won't have to double your walking time! Choose the command words so that they do **not** sound alike, such as "PPC" for one, and "do it—do it" for the other. Later, when you have been using the commands successfully for a couple of months and have probably given the two commands in succession a large number of times, don't be surprised to see that both dogs will respond to either command.

Q. Must I always speak this command softly?

A. No. As soon (in about 3 days) as it is clear to you that the sound of your voice is not disturbing the dog, gradually resume a normal speaking tone and loudness. (But don't shout!)

Timing Diagram

Dog feels urgency—ignores you Circling Sniffing	***Watch***	**L** **O** **O** **S** **E**
Stance Sphincter opens Muscles contract	***Repeat*** ***Command***	**L** **E** **A** **S** **H**
Eliminating	***Soft praise O.K.***	
Sphincter closes Muscles relax Leaves area	***Silence***	

MORE ABOUT PRAISE

If the dog comes bounding happily to you as you are leaving the area, and you respond with praise and affection, you will (by now) understand that you are praising the dog for coming to you on his own. The dog will NOT associate this praise with his elimination. However, if you do such a praise sequence after elimination 50 times (every time you teach, for example) he will soon connect the two events. That is unwise, because you want him to connect this praise only with the actual sphincter opening and active elimination. You also want him to keep his PPC for anyone who walks him —even for the kennel or veterinary attendant, or a stranger or friend, or grandma who walks him while you are ill or away.

You may even want to walk your dog for elimination after a summer shower, when you are dressed in white linen slacks and jacket for a wedding, when that play sequence could be a bit of a liability. So, to keep as much specificity in the elimination routine as possible, don't praise and play after each elimination.

Take your dog outdoors to eliminate when he needs to go. Stay quietly *close enough to him so that you can identify the moment of his highest urgency and sphincter opening.* Softly *speak your trigger phrase* several times in succession. *Use the same trigger for elimination from either the bladder or the bowel. Stop saying the trigger the moment he is obviously eliminating. Do not let your trigger or praise be used when the sphincter is closing or when he has finished.*

When you have managed to use the trigger phrase 50 to 75 times at the proper moment over a period of a week to 10 days, your dog will have a conditioned reflex to eliminate anything contained in his bladder or bowel upon hearing the proper word.

TESTING THE RESULTS

THE first time you test your new command to see if you have accomplished your objective, **be sure the dog needs to eliminate.** Take him out at a time when you know he would normally urinate or defecate. Go swiftly to an area he has used before. Give him a moment or two to begin to sniff, but before he begins to circle give him your command softly once or twice (but no more). Follow him on a loose leash. He should eliminate almost immediately. Praise the sphincter opening softly.

If the command is successful, use it again a few times with the sniffing or urgency patterns in familiar places praising each elimination or sphincter opening. When (in about two days) you are getting consistent results by beginning the trigger word with phases 1 and 2, you are ready to try it in the final form. Just be sure the bladder has some urine in it. (Any dog **will** have some urine in the bladder when he has not eliminated for two hours or more.)

In testing the final and complete establishment of the reflex, you need not wait for any urgency. Just give the command softly but definitely. If you want to alert the dog to you, call his name. Then, when his attention is on you, give the command word a time or two in quick succession. Use the same tone which you have used while teaching. He should begin his circling or sniffing and take up his stance within 30 seconds or less. If your dog does eliminate, you have successfully trained him to piddle and poop on command. If 60 seconds go by without any attempt to eliminate, you do not have a complete conditioned reflex established. Go back and teach some more, or consider carefully what you did not do properly. (I have yet to see a dog who does not learn this in the time described.)

Use the command in his **usual** area in its **finished form** for a few days before trying to make it work in a wholly new or very difficult area.

Varying The Places

Normally, a dog will have been eliminating in several different places on his walks.

However, for some dogs, all teaching will have taken place in *one area*. To fully accommodate these one-place-dogs to a flexible PPC, you will need to do a little teaching (using the finished command) in three different places and at three different times. Once you have had success in three different areas, he will readily respond in all other new areas because the dog will "generalize" after three experiences in different areas, and expect that the fourth and fifth places are like the first three.

Of course, if you were able to teach in three or more areas initially, no special attention need be paid to this "Three Rule." *(For more details regarding this rule, see* Appendix C.)

If a particular new area is one the dog has steadfastly refused to use voluntarily, be sure you take him to it first with a very full bladder or an urgent bowel. The command will then work with such immediacy that the dog will probably not be able to inhibit his new response. Give the command a second time with your usual soft tone if the first time doesn't work. Don't give the dog the feeling that you are "uptight" about the new area. He'll read your anxiety, and it will cancel some of your effort. Be sure to add the usual soft praise when your dog is in the full process of eliminating in this strange area. You may even wish to insert a single soft praise while he is circling or taking up his stance—just suggesting how wonderful he is to start responding.

Both of you may feel especially elated when you succeed, but it would be wise to just act normally about the event, as if it were a nice everyday pattern.

Now that you have taught your dog to eliminate on command, we'll review a few important methods for keeping this purely conditioned reflex (Pavlov Type I) ready and able to function.

SOME SPECIAL RULES ABOUT THE CONDITIONED REFLEX AND ITS USE IN THE DOG

1. Fading. Use the reflex once a day if you can because if it is not used at least every few days, it will become less and less effective and disappear; i.e., it will fade. It may be re-established easily enough by going through some of the conditioning process again, but it is easier just to use it regularly to keep the relationship established.

2. Cancellation. If the command is used several times in a row when the dog **cannot** eliminate, the trigger may have to be reimplanted properly a few times to make up for your errors. In other words, this type of conditioning can be cancelled by inappropriate use of the signals.

3. Interference. If the command is used at too many moments of high excitement, it may be ignored by the dog and cancellation will result. You can reimplant the word again for a day or two to strengthen the pattern.

The Eighteenth Tree

Let's also say a word about the "leg lifter" dog who likes to mark every tree in the forest, even when he hasn't a drop of urine left!

This is marking, not eliminating. It is not to be encouraged! Use the first two or three leg-lifted stances to implant your command. Then do not allow continued "marking" during the walk if you can help it. Firmly clasp your end of the leash against your body with both hands and walk briskly away. The dog will have to follow or fall over! (If you are not walking your dog on a leash, you will not have such easy control to help eliminate this problem.)

The dog normally does not empty his bladder completely the first time. (Also, any dog whose bladder is **very** full may not be able to empty his bladder completely at one time.) You can tell by the amount of urine expelled each time he stops whether "this trip was necessary." Two or three urination acts in succession should be adequate to empty your dog's bladder. You will not want to encourage your male dog to hold back urine for marking purposes.

WHEN MORE THAN ONE PERSON
WALKS THE DOG

When different people walk the dog during the teaching week, one person (the one who will walk the dog most often) should do the initial training. When that person has established the pattern so that it works consistently, another person should use the command each time he walks the dog for a week, just as if he alone were teaching the whole procedure.

During the week the second person is training, the first person should continue to use the trigger word occasionally to get results on walks. (The "Three Rule" is also applicable to different people walking a dog; see *Appendix C.)*

After you have finished training and you have tested and found that each person who may need to use the command is getting consistently good results, you should begin to relax on the number of times the commands are used. You don't have to use the command every time the dog eliminates. If you use it a few times every week and get results, it will stay fresh and clear in the dog's mind and will always be there to use when you need it.

If the dog does not hear the command properly for over two months, it may not work at once.

Don't overuse the command. Don't say it **every** time you take him out. Such repetition could backfire in the following manner: your dog probably has a way in which he presently lets you know he needs to go outside. He **tells** you when it's "necessary now" by some attitude or action you and he have learned together. This important signal he gives helps you to maintain his housebreaking. This pattern was also worked out partly or wholly by "conditioning." (The dog conditioned **you** to respond!) **Don't let useful old patterns fade from disuse. If the dog never needs to tell you, he may forget how to tell you.**

Once you have taught elimination on command, go back to normal living and use the new technique along with all the old communications you have with your dog.

Summary of the Piddle And Poop on Command Sequence

1. Choose the trigger (use a phrase, word, visual signal, or even a touch).

2. Identify the dog's sphincter opening time.

3. Use the trigger phrase 50 to 75 times during sphincter opening.

4. You may praise the dog sometimes when elimination is fully in process. Stop praise before his sphincter closes.

5. Gradually change from a soft tone to a normal tone of confident command.

6. Test and use the command first in familiar places, then in more difficult places.

7. Replace the trigger command if it fades. Don't let this conditioning or any other communications you have with your dog suffer from disuse.

That's all there is to it! It may be the easiest thing the dog ever learned. We hope you'll enjoy the new freedom and comfort PPC will mean for both you and your dog.

APPENDIX A
OUT OF SIGHT

PERHAPS your dog never eliminates where you can see him. It will be necessary for you to find a way to be nearby in order to teach your dog to piddle and poop on command. Find an area your dog frequently uses. Take the dog to that area after keeping him in the house until you know he needs to "go" by his actions. (Don't let him out of your sight while you are in the house waiting for his urge to become **very strong!**) Then quickly, quietly, and easily—don't get excited or uptight—take him to this area, turn your back and walk softly and slowly away. Find the proper distance which is necessary to make him comfortable. From this distance you may softly insert praise words ("good girl," "good boy," "very good") during his elimination. Don't use his name. It is important not to startle him or get his mind involved in appreciating your presence. After a few days of pleasant experience of this type with you, he should allow you to come somewhat closer, or at least require you to walk less far away.

If your dog's problem is more serious, you may confine him in the area he usually uses by setting a long tie rope so that it will be available when you are ready. You might also erect a temporary light fence of chicken wire around one of his chosen areas, so that you can confine him there. When he has a strong need, you can tie him or confine him to the area and pretend to walk away. In this fashion, he cannot run out of your sight, and will gradually accommodate to your increasingly near presence—especially if you gently praise him during his elimination. His hearing is much more acute than yours and mine. He may easily hear your soothing sound from quite a distance. I have seen dogs aware of a master's soft voice from two hundred feet away! (Or was it ESP?)

After the dog has accommodated to your presence and praise, and you are coming closer and closer to him, it will be clear to you when you can begin to use the command words. He should be very mildly aware of the sound of your voice, and of the quality of the trigger sounds themselves. These sounds will then work to create the reflex conditioning, even if he can barely hear them.

APPENDIX B
OFF LEASH

IF your dog will only eliminate off leash, but you wish him to learn to eliminate on leash, you can do it in the following way. Attach a piece of light line to the dog's collar, cut just long enough so that it reaches well behind his front paws as it drags along the ground. This line should have no knots in it. A piece of mason twine or a small piece of venetian blind cord is quite adequate. He may wear it around the house if you wish, without getting into difficulty because it will not catch on furniture or doors. If he drags this line for a few days, he'll get used to it.

(For safety, however, remove the line at night, or when leaving him alone in the home or kennel, and **never** allow him to chew on it.)

A real "No-No"

*What IS that thing I'm
stepping on?*

*It doesn't bother ME
any more — I can
do anything*

Let's go out

You may then follow him about and teach him to eliminate on command while he is dragging his short line. (Use the techniques of Appendix A.) After he has been well taught, tie a six-foot piece of similar line to his collar. Have him drag this line about the house, and out of doors during elimination for the next day or so. You can then pick up the end of the line. By this time you have taught him elimination on command and whether you are holding the line or not, the dog will be able to eliminate. **Don't tighten the line or collar while he is eliminating, or while he is sniffing and getting ready to eliminate.** When he has eliminated for a week or more on command with you holding the line loosely, you will be ready to attach a heavier leash. Holding the leash loosely in the same way you held the lighter line, give your trigger word, and your dog will eliminate while wearing a leash.

He will probably have learned to walk nicely on the leash in this process also. As he drags the line he learns that his own feet produce "tugs" on his collar as he steps on the line, and he quickly learns not to fear those tugs he himself produces. He may have become angry at a leash **you** tugged upon—but he is not likely to become angry at his light line when **he** steps on it. He has also learned that wearing a line means a chance to go outdoors for his comfort. In a sense, he has now conditioned himself to the wearing of a leash, and the tugs it produces on his collar are no longer a signal for rebellion, but an invitation to a walk.

APPENDIX C
BASIC LAWS

METHODS by which this program was constructed:

1. SIMULTANEITY

The dog clearly associates those events and conditions which occur together at the same time. A relaxed atmosphere and a soft tone allow a dog to be aware of this clear association of subtle factors. A major distraction, such as a loud or surprising sound or sensation, can override more subtle perceptions and interfere with subtle learning. (By the same token, loudness or surprises can be used in other training with great benefit when overriding is required, but that is not in any way a part of the training for PPC and must be avoided.)

2. REPETITION

Reflex patterns can be established by approximately fifty repetitions of a simultaneous set of sensations and perceptions.

3. REFLEX MAINTENANCE is achieved
by appropriate use of signals intermittently, by avoiding misuse, and by avoiding cancellation through inappropriate use.

4. THE "THREE RULE"

A dog will "generalize" a rule of action when he has been taught it and obtained experience with it at three different times and in three different places. (For example, a dog will consider your home a "different place" when you are having a party with a houseful of strangers present, and may consider a place "different" when you install a new carpet, or leave him totally alone in a "normally busy" home.)

Until the "Three Rule" has been satisfied, he may be unreliable in a strange new area, and require re-teaching. Teach in several places to gain solidity of training patterns.

(You can tell if you have satisfied his "Three Rule" for generalization with PPC if he reliably eliminates on a single command in strange places.)

EPILOGUE

W HILE talking to an accountant the other day on the telephone, he began discussing a dog of his who had died a few years ago. He seemed remorseful about not getting another dog, but said that he just couldn't go out and stay in the bad weather for long periods of time any more—sub-zero weather, snowstorms, icy sidewalks after a slight thaw.

He said that his dog hadn't slipped around or seemed to get tired of the cold. (Four feet make a big difference in stability!)

His wife had obtained a cat who follows her around the house, and "she's grown to like that cat very much," he told me wistfully. "But it **isn't** as much pleasure as a **dog**," he emphatically added.

I told him I was writing this little book, and his voice brightened.

"You mean that I could teach my dog so that I didn't have to walk long distances in bad weather?" he asked. "I used to come in too soon at times, and then he'd eliminate in the house— which was no good at all as a selling point for my wife."

I assured him that PPC would work for him, too, and now he says he's anxiously awaiting his copy. I'd better get this book to press, because the fall rains are coming, and I've got a feeling he's out hunting for a new puppy already!

the end

*A*CKNOWLEDGMENTS

T HE following individuals, through their personal services, publications, review and criticism of my work and the work of the Foundation for Applied Studies of Animal Behavior have contributed greatly to the success of the teaching methods, and to our understanding of how and why these methods work. Without them I would not know what has been written in these pages, nor have had the testing ground for my ideas.

William R. Koehler
Lillian Koehler
Allen Cosnow, DVM
Edna C. Guibor, DVM
John Paul Scott, Ph.D.
Daniel Cornell, DVM
Marjorie Seymour
L.R.H. Seymour (in memoriam)
Kristy Pokorny
Adrienne Goodman
Richard Goodman
Ed Feinstein
Kris Minnick (in memoriam)
Gale Minnick
Mary Jane Strauch
Joyce Henderson (in memoriam)

and all the dedicated Shepherd House trainers, assistants and the students whose work was crucial to my understanding.

ABOUT THE AUTHOR

D R. Marjorie Smith was born in Springfield, Illinois, and received her undergraduate and medical degrees at Northwestern University and at the University of Illinois College of Medicine, respectively. In addition to conducting basic research projects in neurophysiology and behavior, she was the founder of both the Medical Emergency Services Associates in the Chicago area, and the Illinois Chapter of the American College of Emergency Physicians. She has chaired a number of medical research and training committees during her career, and more recently has served as Program Director of Emergency Medical Services and as Director of the Senior Services in San Juan County, Washington, where she now resides. Among her medical achievements was a successful program to reduce recidivism at the California Institution for Men, a federal prison at Chino, California, using human-dog relationships, conducted under the direction of W. R. Koehler.

Dr. Smith also served as president and chairman of the board of the Foundation for Applied Studies of Animal Behavior in Deerfield, Illinois, and was the founder of the Shepherd House Dog Training Facility in Chicago, now a division of that foundation.